The Power Of

Visualization

How Successful People Use The Power Of The Mind To Achieve Goals And Get Everything They Want In Personal Life And Business

Azione Business

reader will render any resulting actions solely under their purview. There are no scenarios in which the publisher or the original author of this work can be in any fashion deemed liable for any hardship or damages that may befall them after undertaking information described herein.

Additionally, the information in the following pages is intended only for informational purposes and should thus be thought of as universal. As befitting its nature, it is presented without assurance regarding its prolonged validity or interim quality. Trademarks that are mentioned are done without written consent and can in no way be considered an endorsement from the trademark holder.

Table Of Content:

Introduction

We have been programmed from the very moment of our birth.

All those programs we live by right now were given to us when we were very small and we got them from our parents, our teachers, and from all the authority figures we had around us as kids. Even the environment we were born in and grew up with played a big role in who we are now. All this programming received at a very young age still conditions today the choices we make every single day of our lives.

Now, if what surrounds you in your life it is not what you want and you don't like it, or maybe you like it, but you want to improve it, then you have to figure out what it is that is stopping you from getting the results you want.

What is blocking you from getting those successful results it's all the programming you received during your life. All these programs installed in you created mental models that make you repeat always the same actions, and all those repeated actions give you more of those results that you don't like. You can't have different results by doing the same things.

So, to get new results you need to start acting differently, and to do so you have to re-write all those mental programs you have deep down in yourself.

The process that can help you do that is what I call Conscious Visualization. During this process, you have to deliberately create mental pictures of what you want to achieve so that these new images will re-write any old model that is not aligned with your actual desires.

Visualizing is that process by which you bring and hold images on the screen of your mind through your imagination. Imagination is the starting point of every single thing that surrounds you and me, each thing you can see around you started in somebody's head.

The MacBook I am using to write this book was first imagined and then realized. The chair where I am sitting right now was first imagined and then realized.

Imagination is a very strong component to understand and apply visualization in a practical way and it's vital to get the results you truly want. In the next chapter, you will understand how and why.

Chapter 1:

Use Visualization To Improve Yourself

Probably, at this very moment, you are not getting the results you desire, and you keep asking yourself why so many people can get exactly what they want and you don't seem capable to do the same.

When you look around yourself, you get the feeling that everybody else is getting better results than you are. They have a better job, they make more money, they are happier, they are in a relationship with someone they love, they are in better shape. So you keep asking yourself where is it that you are mistaking, what is it that is not working correctly, and why you don't get what you want.

I think that your first step should be to ask yourself better questions. You should be asking yourself: "How can I get what I want?".

By asking the wrong questions you keep focusing on the causes that brought you where you don't want to be. You keep thinking about all the mistakes you made, instead of concentrating on how you could get yourself out of this situation you dislike. You need to start thinking about solutions you can apply to improve the quality of your life.

Visualization can help you with that. I wrote this book to help you apply visualization on a daily basis so that with this method you can start to change every single area of your life that you don't like.

With the help of your imagination, you will start to see things from a new point of view and the solutions you were looking for will start to appear right in front of your eyes.

You will form in your mind new and clear goals and with them, you will start to build something new for yourself and in your life. You will improve all those situations you don't like in your life by applying all the solutions that will appear on the screen of your mind during the visualization process.

Chapter 2:

The Results You Can Get By Applying This Method

I know a lot of people (me included) that got amazing results by applying their imagination and their visualization to reach their goals and their success.

I could mention most of the biggest sports stars. They constantly apply this method. They state the goal: win the competition. Then they start to picture the entire contest on the screen of their minds with full details. They imagine the location in perfect conditions, the weather they desire, the reaction they want the audience to have, and they see in detail their performance, their victory and they feel exactly how they will feel at the moment of the victory on the actual day of the competition.

Another good example is represented by self-made millionaires. The majority of those millionnaires state that they constantly applied visualization to get the success and the wealth that they wanted in their lives. Before they could reach the level of success they desired they had to see it on their minds. They explain that they regularly imagined themselves with all the money they wanted, with all the nice toys they desired, with anything they liked to have. They would focus the visualization on feeling like they already had achieved all that and feeling the sensations of already having the wanted success and wealth.

A lot of people have changed their entire lives thanks to visualization, in many different areas of those lives. Some used it to improve their health or their physical shape. They applied their imagination to see themselves with the body they wanted to have, feeling as they already had it and picturing themselves doing all the necessary actions they needed to do to get the desired results.

I even read a book in which a psychologist used visualization to help some people that presented some cases of mental health problems. He would make them visualize themselves living a better life and, by constantly repeating this exercise, the mental health problems were reduced by a good deal.

Some other people have used the visualization method for business and sales. They see themselves with a signed contract, they imagine a successful transaction, they see their success and how happy they are with their result. They successfully use this method before each sale meeting, with enormous positive results.

Whether we want it or not, we are guided by images, we think in images and so the images create our thoughts. Those thoughts guide our feelings and our beliefs, and those two direct and create our actions. So, by choosing the images we play on the screen of our mind we can shape our physical world.

Anybody can do it, just like the examples I mentioned in this chapter, and you can do it too. If you want, you can get anything you want. It's absolutely possible!

You can achieve new and better results in your life by constantly and consciously applying visualization to overcome your internal blocks and reach your desires.

Chapter 3:

Something Is Stopping You. You Have Internal Resistances

A lot of people think that this "visualization thing" is not for them. They look around themselves and they don't see anybody among their friends and family doing what I talk about in this book. They don't see anybody regularly practicing visualization, they don't know anybody that uses this method to imagine the life they want and then transform that image into reality. So, they judge the method using the people around as a filter.

Unfortunately, they are probably surrounded by unsuccessful people, mediocre people, losers, and, by following that examples, it will be nearly impossible for them to get anywhere near success. You should think about this situation because it could be your own and it could be one of the resistances that are keeping you away from success.

Other people think that they don't have time to waste on "this stuff". They think to be too busy running their businesses, solving problems, dealing with tons and tons of different things. These kinds of people wake up very early in the morning and go to bed very late at night trying to deal with too many different situations. They think in their mind that, if they had to find time to practice visualization regularly, they would have to leave behind a lot of more important things.

The truth is that it's all the other way around. Those people run around all day dealing with many useless situations and facts because they don't have a clear picture of what they want out of life. Sometimes they don't have a picture at all and it's this lack that causes the messy life they live in. This missing image is the reason why they run all day, they never have time for anything, they work very hard, but they never get results, they are always stuck in the same place. This situation brings about a very negative mindset in those people. They keep looking for solutions they can't find, so they start to think that they are not up for it, that they are not as good as other people are and that success will never come for them.

This is another situation that could be your own, so you should seriously think about it, because this could be what is blocking to become successful and from using this technique that could easily grant you all the success you want, in every area of your life.

When we are little children we learn everything we know from our parents, our teachers, from all those people near us that, in some ways, we recognize as authority figures. We learn attitudes, behaviors, even how to think. But, because we learned it from so important for us, it doesn't mean it's all correct. For example, we learn to confront ourselves with other people. This causes the thought that we have to be like the majority, similar to the average person, to be similar to everybody else.

Look around you, 99% of people you encounter every day are upset, unhappy, unhealthy, complaining all the time about something. You don't want to be one of them. So, what you have been thought of as real, is not. We were told that everybody does this or that and you have to follow the same path because this is the reality we live in. "Go to school, the take a loan to go to university, look for a job, get married, take a mortgage for a house and a couple of loans for the cars,...", because this is the reality, this is what everybody else does.

Well, this is a lie! This is not the reality at all, somebody decided to call it so, just because the majority acts that way. The reality, the true reality is the one that **you decide** to create for yourself, every moment of every day.

When we confront ourselves with the so-called reality, we usually don't like it at all. We hate the job we are in, we hate all the debts we have and many other things, but we carry along that path because somebody has told us to do so. What I find funny is that, sometimes, we don't even remember who told us a certain thing, but we keep living by it.

So, when as kids somebody told us what to do, how to do it, how to be in life, that person created in our mind thoughts, ideas, feelings, emotions, that have conditioned our entire life. That person created our way of doing things, our way of thinking, of choosing, and all this creates our reality.

So, the reality you are living just now and the results you are getting are not your own. With the method that I am explaining in this book, you have the chance to change everything.

Here is my question for you, "What if all those things we were thought were wrong?".

Chapter 4:

With Commitment And Dedication, You Will Soon See Your First Results

Many people have to face all the problems, blocks, and resistances that I described in the previous chapter to reach success, and a lot of them reach outstanding results by applying this method.

If you want proof, bookstores are full of books written by ordinary people that reached amazing success, biographies of people that realized all their dreams.

When you read those books you clearly understand that everybody's path is full of problems, that you just have to keep on going despite all obstacles. In most cases, success and happiness were right behind the last corner and so these people reached their success through their commitment and their dedication to go on despite the problems.

You have to keep in mind that whatever you are doing right now, or you will be doing in the future, you will always face problems. Success is going on despite all problems and roadblocks you will encounter along your path. You don't have to consider these issues as permanent, there always is a way around them. Most of the time we don't see any solution and we feel very down about it, but all you need is something or someone that shows you things from a different perspective and the solution will appear right in front of your eyes. Allow yourself to see these new points of view.

You will always face problems when you set a goal for yourself and the says of the issues will be proportional to the size of the goal you set for yourself: the bigger the goal, the bigger the troubles.

Let's analyze some famous examples. Take Thomas Edison, the inventor. He failed about 6000 times before inventing the light bulb, but he didn't care, because he had a vision of himself inventing the light bulb. He used all his commitment and dedication to manifest his mental image in the real world.

Another good example could be Henry ford with the V8 Engine invention. Nobody had ever built a V8 Engine before, but he could see it in the screen of his mind. So he called his best engineers and told them to develop this ambitious project. After a year they had come up with nothing, but Ford told them he didn't care, they just had to carry on trying. After other six months of trials the engineers made it and the rest is history, but the true point here is that with dedication and commitment he materialized his vision.

All you need is an image, and with dedication and commitment, you can materialize it in your life, too.

Chapter 5:

What I Didn't Know At The Beginning

A few years ago, when I started practicing martial arts, I was looking for a way to improve my performance. I was looking for a solution to perform at my best every time and on every occasion. It was very important for me to find a way because I was doing martial arts both for pleasure and for work, in fact, I was a martial arts instructor. I had to be always at my best and, because it was a contact martial art, I had to be always well trained and concentrated, to avoid physically painful situations. Also, teaching this discipline I had to be better than the students in my class.

I used to spend long hours every day training myself, and it was hard sometimes because, after a few hours of training energies start to lower. I read a lot of books about Bruce Lee in that period, I discovered that he would train 4, 6 even 8 hours a day and I wanted to perform that way too, but I wasn't capable.

I couldn't keep my concentration for such long times to train myself efficiently. I couldn't find a way to get the best results with the least effort until I discovered visualization.

After a few years, I created my first business. I started pretty much from zero, I knew nothing about owning a business, I knew very little about that kind of business I was getting myself into, so I could say I had nearly no experience. I decided that my first step was studying. I started looking for people with successful businesses in the area of my concern and I started listening to what they had to say about it. I search for what those people were doing to improve themselves and their businesses. Day after day I was learning new pieces of informations. The more I learned the more a clear image was starting to take shape in my mind. I could see how I wanted my business to be, what kind of results I wanted from it, what I would have done to get all I wanted. I imagined everything in every single detail and this is exactly what happened. My vision turned into reality.

Another personal example I can share about the power of visualization it's from the period of my life in which I decided I wanted to make an experience as a salesman. It was a difficult challenge because I had never sold anything before and I didn't have a clue on where to start.

After a few days on the job, I started to ask myself how I could perform better because I wasn't doing well at all. So I started to read books, take sales classes and train myself with customers, but I wasn't getting anywhere near the results I wanted.

I started talking to people, looking for suggestions, but the majority of them answered with a way of saying very popular in Italy, "If you were not born a salesman, you will never become one".

Now, I can say it's one of the dumbest sentences I have ever heard and I know I was talking to the wrong people but, at that time, it disappointed me a lot.

I thought there was something wrong and I couldn't grasp what. Looking around me, I could see some people reaching amazing levels of performance and others failing miserably. Why was that? I needed to understand the reason.

What helped me make the big switch was the word "performance" which was in common with my previous experience in martial arts. This word gave me the input to start using in sales the same method I had used to improve in my martial arts training. My purpose was the same in both cases, I needed a performance improvement, so I thought to try this path, again.

I started looking if somebody already tried this method in sales and I studied those persons. A clear picture started to take form in mind, I started to see my sales success and how I could reach it. I started to apply and, once again, my vision turned into reality. I got amazing results in a very brief space of time.

Chapter 6:

How I Discovered Visualization

When I began to practice martial arts I started going to book stores very frequently. I would look for books on different subjects that could help me improve my performance. So I started to read books on psychology and meditation, on focus and concentration, manuals about training, and biographies of top athletes who reached outstanding success.

A book, in particular, caught my attention. It was an anthology of success stories about athletes in different disciplines and how they reached the top. The book told stories about runners, swimmers, skiers, but the one that caught my deepest attention was a man practicing free diving. This guy would go very deep down the sea without scuba tanks, just with the air he had in his lungs. I found that truly amazing.

What I found even more interesting were his training techniques. In fact, he had a lot of different training methods because he had to prepare his body for the huge effort, but his mind needed training just as much if not even more, to support the body's efforts.

I found one of those methods was particularly worthy of my attention. He would put himself in a state of total relaxation, he would then go into a meditation state and then he would start to see his entire performance on the screen of his mind. He would visualize the event in every single detail, even the smallest.

The vision was clear as if it was real: he saw himself diving underwater, he felt his muscles' reactions, he pictured everything that could happen and how he would react, etc. He would picture and clearly see every single aspect of his performance, long before it took place. And, of course, his results were amazing, outstanding.

Wow! This was my breakthrough! This was the solution I was looking for and I immediately understood I needed to master this visualization discipline to get the results I wanted. So I started hunting for books and materials on this subject.

I read books about the mind, visualization, and meditation. I would look for articles and materials on the internet. Most of them were in English and I am Italian, so I had to translate them before I could study what they were saying.

After all my studying and reading I started to practice relaxation, control my breathing, and meditate just as all those materials suggested. When I got in the right state I would try to imagine most efficiently the results I wanted to get. Step-by-step my image would take shape in my mind in full detail. I could clearly see it.

The more I was studying and practicing the various aspects of the process, the better I felt. My training performance was definitely improving, but I could see a beneficial effect on everything else I was doing. My focus and concentration were higher than usual, I was calm and I could control my body and my reactions a lot better than ever before.

When I stopped teaching martial arts, I kept practicing them and I kept practicing visualization in that contest. As I mentioned in the previous chapter, events lead me to apply the visualization process to sales. My results after applying this method went sky high, I sold 100.000 euros in pretty cheap products, for the company I was working for, in a single month (ranking first salesman for many months).

After those events, I started applying visualization to everything I do and I never stopped practicing it. I still practice it on daily basis and this is how this book came to be.

Chapter 7:

Let's See How You Get Benefits Out Of It

"I visualize, but it doesn't work!".

I hear this sentence very often, but the truth is that you either don't recognize the benefits or you didn't give visualization enough time to develop your path.

Let's say, for example, that you started visualizing to solve a problem. For how long have you had this problem in your mind? Do you know what happened? For all that time you have been unconsciously practicing negative visualization.

It could be one year that you have a problem at work, so it's one year that your mind is buzzing with what doesn't go well in your work. You think about it, you create ideas in your mind about it, you create pictures and develop negative emotions. Your mind has been filled for most of your day for nearly one year with what you don't want.

You practiced negative visualization unconsciously for one year. Your mind is full of negative thoughts and ideas that eventually generated negative emotions. You held those emotions inside yourself long enough to generate actions dictated by those feelings. Those actions created and reinforced your negative believes on that matter and so, you keep getting a result you don't want.

To solve your problem, you have to recreate the same process by positively using visualization, by visualizing what you what. You start and you desire to see things change in a few days of practicing. Unfortunately, it doesn't work that way, you have to give the process a little time. After all, you stayed on negative visualization for a year, I am sure you can stay on the positive one a little more than a bunch of days.

The good news is that the energy of positive visualization is a lot stronger than the negative one, so you won't need a year to get rid of your problem, but you will surely need a little more than a handful of days.

The length of time needed depends on the intensity of your positive visualization. You have to fill your head with what you want and keep it occupied just with that. Visualize the ideal and positive scenery you want to live in and hold it on the screen of your mind all the time. You may not materialize it exactly as you see it, but you will get close enough, in fact, things will start to happen that drive you in the direction of your mental picture.

For example, if your problem at work is your colleagues, visualization may not make disappear your horrible colleagues, but you could get a better job opportunity in a team of amazing people.

Sometimes, when I travel around to do seminars and speeches on how to get your goals through visualization, I hear a lot of people talking about will as a means to get results. In particular, they wonder how they could get such amazing results through visualization if they couldn't get any through the strength of their will.

"I make huge efforts, but it doesn't work". "I keeping trying harder, without any result". "I keep pushing myself to act more and more, but nothing changes".

These are just a few examples of what I hear people saying. Here is what I understood in years of studying and practicing this discipline: in a face to face between will and imagination, imagination always wins and will is the loser.

There are two reasons why I believe this. First, you can only try so much harder, at some point your will loses its strength. For example, if you are on a diet, after a long day at work, in the evening when you sit down at your dinner table, you will probably indulge more than you should, because you lost strength during the day and it's a lot harder to resist to temptations.

Second, when you deal with the will, the harder you try the harder it gets because you create a sort of tension. It's like when you go to bed and you can't sleep. You keep trying to fall asleep, you get agitated because sleep is not coming, and then you can't sleep because you are too tense and agitated. You should just let everything go, relax, sleep will come to you and so will your results.

Other factors may obstacle your results with visualization. They may come from your environment, in fact, we are very much influenced by people we hang around with, places in which we spend time, and from all the pieces of information that we gather through our senses.

All those factors develop a series of thoughts in our minds, those thoughts develop feelings and emotions and, at this point, we start to build beliefs. We live our lives following our beliefs.

This simple process takes place without us even noticing it, it's natural. It happens at a subconscious level, automatically, without any effort. We don't need to try harder or be forceful, it just happens.

We usually don't filter what we get from the environment, it just gets in by the simple process I just described and, once we have built our belief, we act by that. Those actions don't bring us the results we want, so we think that the solution is to try harder and to impress strength to this process to achieve the desired changes. Unfortunately, the problem sits elsewhere and so you make a double mistake.

If you force your strength of will on this method you create a situation that is exactly the opposite of what it should be. This forceful attempt goes against the nature of the method with which you build you believes. So you don't impress anything in your subconscious mind, and nothing changes.

To create new beliefs that can make you act in a new way to get new different results, you have to keep yourself in a neutral and "relaxed" state. In this way, the process can do its natural course. The important thing is to do the process for what you want and to do so you have to carefully choose the information that you accept in your life, wherever they may come.

Did you get both mistakes? The first one is the attempt to force the system and the second one is the lack of choice of the information you let in your mind.

So, all you need to do is to chose properly what you want to allow into your mind and then let the process do its course. Then, through visualization, you can reinforce the process. You can imagine in full detail what you truly want, connected to the idea you accepted into your mind, and you have to do this visualization in a totally relaxed state. Every idea you reject has to stay out of your mind and off your visualization forever.

This is how you can get your goal through visualization, this is how you impress in your subconscious mind what you want and then your subconscious will express it into actions that will lead to the desired result. There is no need to be forceful, just relax and start visualizing what you really want.

When I talk about how important is to relax in visualization I get a huge amount of people telling me that they can't visualize because in such a noisy world they cannot find a quiet spot to practice and sometimes it's even hard to find the time.

This is, of course, an excuse. It's their old paradigm trying to stop them (you will understand this better in a further chapter). Anyhow, if you are one of them there are two easy solutions that I always share with these people, too.

First, wait for all your family to go to bed and then reserve 15 or 20 minutes just for yourself, in a silent house where everybody else is sleeping and can't disturb you. Sit down in a comfy position and start your visualization.

Second, get up in the morning 15 or 20 minutes before anybody else. Same situation as described for the night. In a silent house with everybody still asleep, sit down in a comfy position and start to visualize. You can even alternate, sometimes morning, sometimes nighttime. The important thing is to create a little time just for yourself.

If for some reason, you can't get a silent place where to relax and do your practice, and any minimal noise disturbs your concentration and you can't relax, use earplugs. I do, I use them all the time. I put my earplugs on and I relax in total silence. I buy 3 pairs for about 9 euros and I think it's a great amount of money to buy the silence.

Chapter 8:

How Do I Put It Into Practice

I am not a doctor, I am a person that likes to look for solutions. I like to study, to try and apply, and to see if I can reach the desired solution.

I met visualization in 1997, and I have been practicing it ever since because I immediately understood the enormous results I could get by applying it to my everyday life. Ever since I started to use this method, I have been trying to improve it to get better results in my own life.

In this chapter, I want to share and explain exactly how I use visualization in my own life. I want to show what, in my opinion, works better, what you can change or improve with this technique, what "tools" you can use to get better and where I got my best results, and in which areas I recon you can apply it.

Visualization is a huge subject, and I want to encourage you not to stop with this book. You should go in major depth with other books, scripts, articles, courses. I still do so myself, and I think this is the best way to find a method totally suitable for yourself to get the best results.

Before getting to the exact practice of the method I would like to clarify some aspects that I recon should know very well to properly understand how and why visualization is so effective. I believe that, if you don't know these concepts very well, you could trace wrong and misleading conclusions.

I will try to be brief and to treat these concepts in the easiest way possible. Once you will get comfortable with them, the all visualization process and why you should use it to improve your actual situation will become clear and easier to comprehend.

1. Your Convictions

A conviction is an opinion, a very well rooted idea, or a principle of which you are certain.

There two types of convictions: conscious and unconscious. If we know we have a conviction, we recognize its existence, we have a conscious conviction. Most frequently, we don't even know to have a certain conviction, it's subconscious, very well buried inside us.

Those are the most dangerous ones and they can cause us a lot of problems. They determine a limit that stops us from reaching our goal and we don't even notice or realize it.

Most of those subconscious convictions were planted in our subconscious minds when we were just young children. We got them from our parents and from the environment around us at that time. We accepted them as good because we didn't have the ability to chose if they were good or bad for us.

The problem is that today we carry on acting by those old and wrong convictions, without even realizing it, this leads us to results we don't want and we don't even know why that happens.

The good news is that you can change your convictions by repeating new information and visualization is a great means for doing so.

2. Your Beliefs

Beliefs are thoughts that we consider to be true. We create those truths by tapping into the information we already have in our mind or that we perceive through our senses.

What we call and define as truth or reality, it's just our point of view. I believe in God because my experience and my perception of reality tell me that there is an Energy in the universe that I call God. So, I believe in God because I recognize that the energy of the universes true for me.

Let's take an easier example. I see a couple sitting on a bar table, a man and a woman. They talk, but I can't hear the conversation. She starts crying, then she gets up and leaves the bar.

My mind starts a process, I start creating ideas. Maybe he just left her, they broke up. My previous experiences determine my thoughts. Maybe they are related and they were just sharing sad family news.

Depending on what I believe to be the truth of the situation, I will act. I might go after the woman to see if she needs any help, or go and talk to the guy left alone to see if he needs any support.

Whatever action I take is dictated by what I believe and how I read the scene I just observed. The same happens in your everyday life. You act by the input that you receive from your beliefs, but they may be incorrect, and they are incorrect if you are not reaching the goal you set.

You can change your beliefs and to do so you need to deeply analyse yourself. Why do you do certain things instead of others? Why do you believe that thing is right or wrong? Why do you believe in a certain thing?

Try to understand what beliefs you have that are stopping you from doing those actions that could lead you to reach your goal. Then understand which beliefs can lead you to act towards your goal and install them in your subconscious mind through repetition and visualization. Those new beliefs will become soon very strong thanks to the process of understanding you went through to build them.

3. Your Fears

Fear is an emotion.

It is a very important emotion that you need to learn how to control because sometimes it can save your life, but in most cases, it will be an obstacle toward a bright future.

There two kinds of fear: real fears and imaginary fears. If a get hunted by a tiger in the middle of the jungle, this fear is very real. The fear to get killed will be very useful for me and it will dictate my next actions to save my life.

If you are planning to open up a business and you start wondering what would people think about you, you will start fearing their judgment, fearing to make mistakes. This fear is not real, it's not there, it's just in your imagination, but you will act consequently. Actually, you would probably not act at all, stopped by something that doesn't even exist.

You should not be giving fear the power to stop you, otherwise, you will never reach your goal. The problem is that we don't recognize our fears. We see them always as real, even when they are not.

What really happens is that you think about your goal and then you start using your imagination to see the worst possible scenario, those images you created in your mind seem very real and scary and they generate the negative emotion of fear.

To overcome fear, stop focusing on being unsuccessful. Instead, start using visualization to see your success, start building wonderful images that will generate amazing and positive emotions.

4. Paradigms

Paradigms are a multitude of beliefs, convictions, ideas, and habits that live inside us.

Paradigms are programs that you have in your subconscious mind and they tell you how to do a certain thing. You are born with some paradigms and you develop others along the path of life. For example, you speak a certain language depending on where you are born. On the other hand, you tie your shoes in a certain way because you were thought that way as a child, you have been programmed to tie your shoes that way.

Your logic is dictated by your paradigms, by those programs you have installed in your mind during your life. The way you perceive facts, circumstances and reality comes from this inner programming, it's given by your paradigms. A paradigm tells you to perceive a certain thing in a certain way. This way to perceive a certain thing, this paradigm, is formed by all the information you hold on that subject and that you keep repeating to yourself. You repeated them so often and they stayed in your head for so long that in the end you took them for good and they became your truth, your reality.

Paradigms become a set of rules you live by and they determine two main circumstances. First, they determine your boundaries. Second, they tell you exactly how to think and act inside those boundaries.

Basically, you live by those rules and you will never do any action outside this scheme, so you only live and act inside the boundaries those rules determine.

If you look around you it's easy to see this in action. The majority of people accept and act by those rules, it's this set of rules they have that determines their reality. The paradigms tell them how to see things.

They go to school, then to university, then they start job hunting, they get married, get a mortgage for a house, have kids, and so on. People live this way because they have been told to do so and so many times that this becomes their paradigm. They don't do it because it's what they want and so they don't get the results they want. What about you?

To get the results you want you need to change your paradigms and you can do it by abandoning your old rules and building new ones, through repetition and visualization.

You have to pay a lot of attention to these schemes because they could be so old and so deeply rooted in your subconscious mind that they could represent a huge roadblock on your path for your success.

You should investigate your actions to determine your paradigms and your mental scheme, so you can use the method explained in this book to overwrite old and useless paradigm and start living with a new set of rules, functional towards your success.

5. Your Resistance

Resistance is something that blocks you e prevents you from getting the results you want.

It could be external, for example, a person trying to stop you in any way. It could also be internal, for example, an idea that stops you from acting in the way you need to get your goal.

Resistance can be real or it can be just fictitious. For example, a member of your family trying to stop you from working at your goal it's real. The idea that you can't be successful it's just fictitious because you can reach any goal you set. In fact, you might have created this idea over time looking at facts in the wrong way, you may perceive it like it's true, but it's not.

Analyze yourself and your results. Try to determine a list of resistances you may have: people trying to stop you, giving you unrequested pieces of advice, ideas that stop you from acting, ...

If you know your resistances you can work to eliminate them from your path to success.

6. Your Limits

Limits are like a mental fence that you think you can not climb over, or maybe somebody has told you so.

This happens because people around you keep saying that a certain thing has always been done in a certain way and so that's the only way to do it. You believe them and so, if they say something can't be done, you think it's true.

Many times this fence is created around you to protect you from delusion. For example, your dad telling you to get a job in a good office instead of following your dreams it's a fence to protect you from the delusion of failure.

If you want to reach your goal, you need to get out of that fence, you don't need it anymore. So, identify your limits and get ready to overcome every one of them so you can reach your success.

7. Your Emotions

I read a lot of definitions for the word "emotion", but the most suitable for me it's:

Emotion=E-Motion (Energy into Motion)

The way I see this definition is that emotions control us. They control our thoughts and our actions if we let them flow freely. If you don't control your mind with positive emotions, negative emotions will control your mind and ruin your life.

If you let your mind run free without any form of control, it's like a horse without a harness, free to run wherever it wants to. If we don't constantly control our mind filling it with positive emotions, our mind will get all the emotions from the environment and they are mostly negative ones. Hatred, envy, preoccupation, stress, sadness will be what your mind will get all day. In case you don't believe me, just look around you: tv, newspapers, news, ... they spread all those negative emotions everywhere all day long.

If you don't pay attention, you will live, reason, and think all day, every day submerged by those negative emotions that obviously influence every aspect of your life.

We keep complaining that things don't work out. Of course, they don't! With all that negativity in your mind, where do you think you can go?

You have to focus on positive emotions such as joy, love, passion, enthusiasm, gratitude, happiness,... You have to implement all the positive emotions into your visualization. Feel the joy for reaching your goal as it was already real, feel the gratitude for it. This is how you can change thing, through positive emotions.

When you attach your mental images to positive emotions you create a new belief in yourself about what generated that emotion. This idea is fundamental, you must understand it to make the visualization process work for you.

8. Your Habits

Habits are very important because thanks to them your brain doesn't need to make continuous efforts.

Some habits are very useful for us to reach our goals, others are obstacles.

You have to practice visualization, and repeat your practice on a daily basis, so it will become a habit and then you will practice it effortlessly. This is a fundamental habit to reach your goals.

Here is how it works. Mostly everything we do is dictated by habits and many of those things we didn't even like in the beginning. We still don't really like them, but we act on habit.

For example, think about smoking. It's a really stupid thing, whether you smoke tobacco or an electronic cigarette. Your body doesn't need any kind you smoke, you just start to be cool with your friends and other similar silly reasons. I know very well what I am talking about because a long time ago I used to smoke. When you start smoking, the first puffs and the first cigarettes are very painful, but you force yourself to carry on until it stops hurting because it becomes a habit.

We need to use this brain ability to develop habits to our advantage and apply it to positive situations like the practice of visualization.

So, to reach your goal through visualization you have to practice it daily and repeat this action until it becomes a habit that will support you all your life long.

9. Your Values

Our values are all those things we consider truly important in our life. You need to know your own values because they guide you toward your results. What you get in life is determined by your values.

If you like buying shoes and clothes, if you take really good care of your external appearance, this is a clear signal that we value very much the way we appear to the eyes of those people around us. I am not judging here, I am not saying it's right or wrong, because it's neither or. It's just an example to show that you can identify your values through the actions you repeatedly make.

If you take daily care of what you eat, what you drink, if do physical activity every day, you meditate a couple of times a day and you cultivate other healthy habits, this means that your health and the wellbeing of your body are very important for you. Your value is to have a well fit and healthy body.

If you spend every day trying to improve the products you sell, to make them more interesting for the market, if you keep looking for new solutions for your customers, then your value is to improve your business and make more money.

Analyze your actions and try to develop a list of your values, you will find those information useful to know when building your images to visualize.

10. Your Self-Image

Your self-image it's the image you hold of yourself, a sort of opinion you have of yourself and it can be positive or negative. The forming of this imaging is conditioned by the environment we live in, but also by the people we hang around with: parents, family, friends, teachers, …

The way those people interact with us influences our thoughts, their attitude towards us conditions our way of thinking about ourselves. We build mental images to justify their way to behave with us.

If you are surrounded by people that think that you are silly, stupid, and weak and they treat you as you were, you will develop this belief and you will build an image of yourself that will confirm these opinions. Think about a child, when he's really young doesn't seem too strong, maybe growing up he doesn't do very well at school, and the feedback he gets from parents and teachers is that he is weak and stupid, he gets treated like one, that's the image he will develop about yourself and that image will dictate the results of his entire adult life, unless he understands all this and takes action to solve it.

On the other hand, if you live in a positive environment and everybody around you thinks you are a genius, they will treat you like one, you will be influenced by this situation and you will create a self-image of a very smart and capable person.

Our self-image creates our identity. This image is always in motion and it can improve or get worst.

If you do something and it goes wrong, and you let negative thoughts and negative judgments get to you, then you are damaging your image with the consequent detriment of your future.

So, you need to take really good care of your self-image. Don't let failure influence what you think about yourself, stay away from people treating you badly, stay away from all those who try to belittle you. Remember, you already have inside yourself all you need to become successful, realize your dreams, and reach your goals.

It is time for you to create a beautiful, powerful and successful self-image to plant in your subconscious mind through visualization.

What To Do Now

Step 1: Goals to reach or roadblocks you want to get out of your path

Your first step is to decide what you truly want. You need to know your goal, knowing where you are going it's the only way to get there.

I recommend you to evaluate well your goals, especially when you are a beginner with the visualization method. You want to pick a goal that keeps you involved without draining out all your energy. If you set a goal too ambitious for the timeframe you decide to reach it by and then you fail to reach it by that time you may draw incorrect evaluations. For example, you could start thinking that you can't be successful or that it's a goal too ambitious for you, so you start feeling down and upset about yourself.

When you get familiar with this method you understand that all you have to do is to ignore these negative emotions and carry on to reach your goal giving yourself a little extra time. Until then, I recommend you start visualizing smaller goals. In this way, you can see easily see your first results and they will increase your confidence in practicing visualization. The more you get confident, the more your goals can grow in importance and size.

If you have a clear goal, but you feel you have something inside that is stopping you from reaching it, you can use visualization to overcome this resistance and remove the obstacle that is blocking your path.

For example, let's say you are a salesman, you have a clear goal and you know you can achieve it, but you realize that with a certain kind of customers you get stuck, you don't manage to perform the way you usually do and you can't do your presentation and close a contract. In this case, you need to remove whatever is blocking you from interacting properly with that category of clients or customers. Speaking from a practical point of view, you have to train yourself by visualizing a scene in which you show an amazing sales presentation exactly to that group of difficult customers. You have to do it as often as possible and in full detail. See yourself talking to them, see how well you respond to their questions and objections, see how they compliment you for your amazing presentation, and see them signing your contracts. When you do it so many times in your mind, becomes a lot easier to do it in your everyday life. It's like an actor rehearsing for his role.

Sit down in a quiet spot, write down a list of goals you wish to achieve. Pick the one that seems the easiest to you and focus just on that one (keep the list to pick a new goal when this one is achieved). Use this goal to practice and to start to understand how this method works and what amazing results you can easily get out of it.

Step 2: Analyze

You have to constantly analyze if what you decided to visualize is aligned with what you want to achieve.

Think about the image you are creating. How can you improve the image? How can you make it more powerful? Try to understand if a picture works better than the other one by analyzing the feelings and emotions you get from each image.

Before you actually start to visualize you should ask yourself a lot of questions to create the perfect movie on the screen of your mind. Remember, the film you are creating needs to be extremely clear.

Do you like the pictures you are creating? Do you like them 100% or could you do better? Is there something you could add? What details could improve your creation? Music? Light? Sounds from nature?

Sometimes I get suggestions during my meditation. I sit down in a quiet place, I relax completely, I pick an interesting subject and then I let my mind run freely. Then I analyze some of the thoughts that I saw passing through my mind, I check where they come from, if they are any good for me and if they could be good suggestions for my visualization.

Start to create mental pictures and analyze them.

Step 3: Environment

The environment is fundamental! You need a quiet place where you can sit down, relax, and practice your visualization without anything or anybody to disturb you. It would be great if you could always use the same spot.

You should find a quiet spot in your house, a place free from every noise. If you can't find any such place, remember to buy a few pairs of earplugs. I switch off all light, I seek total darkness.

If you live with someone ask them to be quiet for about 20 minutes and ask to be left alone and undisturbed during that time. If it's an understanding person you can easily explain what you are doing and share this life-changing exercise. Many times it won't be possible to explain, because many people find strange things like meditation or visualization. I believe they are missing a big piece that could improve their lives, but whether they understand it or not the important thing is that they let you practice in peace.

Step 4: Relax

One of the basic parts of this process is this: Relax!

You can't get results if you don't relax and let it go. You can call it meditation if you like. What do I mean by meditation? I am talking about a state of total calm both physical and mental. Release your muscles from every tension and free your mind from every thought that is oppressing you. Let your thoughts run freely, let them pass by and flow without stopping them.

It is fundamental to remember that in this phase you have to abandon the use of the strength of your will, as we mentioned before. I know most people will tell you that to reach your goal you will need all the strength of your will you can get, but all the results you will ever get are given by the subconscious, and the subconscious works in a very relaxed state. No tension, no strength.

Of course, it's your will that gets you started. It's the will that tells you it's time to change and to find a way to do it, to hold until you find a way. After that, you have to relax because everything that enters into your subconscious gets there when you are totally relaxed. The new programs for your subconscious will get there without the use of your will.

To change your results you need to change the images you have in your subconscious mind, that's why visualization is so important. To make sure you are sending those images into your subconscious mind you have to be extremely relaxed.

What I do, practically speaking, is to close my eyes in a quiet place and take three long and deep breaths. Then, I slowly count from 10 to 0 while I keep breathing deeply and slowly. As I do this I talk to my body and my breath and I tell them to let go, to release every tension, and to be more and more relaxed. This is the same process I follow when I want to get into a meditation state.

Step 5: Create your movie and visualize it

If you think about your refrigerator, can you see it on the screen of your mind?

If you think about your living room, can you imagine it?

If you think about your kitchen, can you see it?

If you think about your car, can you create a mental picture?

Of course, you can, and this is exactly your starting point for visualizing what you want to materialize in your life. You have to create a mental photo and then, step-by-step, transform this single picture into a movie of the life you really want to live.

You could even create what I call a "mental gym". It's a special place in your mind, a sort of temple, where you go to seek what you are looking for, or just to sit down and watch your movie projected on a big screen.

Ideally, in your movie, you should imagine yourself in the situation you would like to live in real life like you already have achieved it. You should see yourself already in the desired environment, already in possess of the results you want. The more detailed are your pictures the better will be your results. By details I mean to involve all your sense and emotions: smells and perfumes around you, sounds in your ideal surroundings, how would you feeling that situation, and so on.

Many people tell me that they can't see all this stuff. It may be true at the beginning because you probably forgot how to use your imagination. It's ok, you will get better day after day as long as you begin somewhere. You could even just start by closing your eyes and thinking about your goal. Time and training will help you clear your mind and build your amazing movie.

Sometimes we encounter things we don't rationally understand, we don't see how they work, so we don't think they can help us in any way. However, we would feel the benefits if we would only just give it a try.

This is the case, you may not understand how this all works. Well, give it a try! Start practicing anyway and start right away.

Step 6: Statements

Statements are claims to which we attribute a profound certainty. "I am beautiful". "I am smart". "I am very good at this... and that..." and so on.

It is very important to notice if you say these words to yourself during your visualization, how you say those words and how many times. Statements have a huge power to affect your imagination.

This truth also means that you have to be really careful to maintain your claims always positive. If you use negative claims and statements when you talk to yourself or about yourself, things like "I am stupid, useless and I am a loser", you will end up believing them even if they aren't true and you will do yourself a very bad service.

I will go in-depth about statements in a further chapter, just now focus on using positive statements during your visualization and repeat them often in your mind so that your visualization gains strength.

Step 7: Repetition

Repetition is fundamental in this process.

Anything you do continuously and constantly sets your actions. If you are continuously exposed to images, words, and situations they inevitably condition you and your way of acting. We may not notice it, but this is an ongoing process.

Repetition is fundamental even for the visualization process if you want to get results. If you think about it, everything you know you have learned it by repetition, either yours or by people around you keep repeating the same words and actions.

Think about the refrain of a song. It's repeated so many times that you end up learning it by heart and ten years later it's still there, you still remember it.

This is how our mind works. Through the repetition of external inputs, we create ideas. We keep thinking about those ideas, we accept them and so they penetrate into our subconscious. It's the subconscious that tells us how to act, so we act on the ideas we just allowed to penetrate in the subconscious and this is where our results come from.

So, the more we concentrate on something and the more we repeat it, the more our results will be linked to that idea may it be good or bad. Keep that in mind and use it to your advantage.

Build a marvelous movie of your goal and run it on the screen of your mind as often as you possibly can.

Step 8: It's time to act

Nothing happens without action!

It's useless to do all this visualization work if you don't start to do something, even just tiny actions inspired by what you daily visualize. If you thought that all you had to do was to create a mental picture and keep visualizing it, I am sorry to disappoint you: I have to get going!

Maybe, if you lay down on your couch visualizing to lose weight and you don't get up to get food you would eventually lose weight (along with your health), but in all other cases, you have to get moving. The couch example is sarcastic, in case it wasn't obvious.

Through visualization you clarify to yourself the work that needs to be done to reach your goal, you get better ideas and your project gains strength. Nothing exists without action of some sort.

To explain this concept better, I would like to use a very famous example. Somebody I met during my readings that, in my opinion, utilized visualization in an impressive way was Tesla. He would build an entire project completely in his head, no need to write anything down. He would see something on the screen of his mind and he would start picturing how it would work, the possible results, what changes he could apply. The whole project was in his head, but he was also very good at bringing those visualizations into the physical world. He would take all the necessary actions to apply what he just imagined until he could old his invention into his hands. People usually find Tesla a little mysterious, because he didn't leave a lot of written stuff about his inventions and projects. That's because his main lab was his mind.

So, get going! If this concept it's not clear enough, I can tell you right away that you won't get any benefit from what you read up until now. If you don't start acting, you just entertained yourself by reading this book. However, I hope this book is your chance to change and improve your life and I seriously wish you take the first step.

All you need to materialize your visualization in the physical world it's a little step and then all the rest will become clearer to your mind, and all the next step will come to you. If you are visualizing yourself as a rich book author, then start writing a little every day. If you see yourself as the owner of a big company selling services, start producing the materials you see yourself selling in your mental image. If you see yourself launching an amazing product on the market, start working at that product you pictured in your head. Step-by-step the rest of the path will appear in front of your eyes, but you need to start.

It's very important to develop the process correctly so you can keep your mind focused on positive thoughts. Your thoughts need to be in harmony with your actions and when you do something you have to see your success.

Let's say you are working on improving your business, you start adding new services or products, but at the same time, you keep repeating to yourself "I'm not going to make it, it will be a failure", that's exactly what you will get, a failure because the positive impact of you actions will be canceled by the power of your negative thoughts. Maybe you will stop the test of a product too soon or you will do the wrong choices on marketing the new product because your negative internal dialogue will influence you, without you even know it.

Step 9: Time

How long does it take for this method to show the first results? I get asked this question so often. This is a very important subject and it would take a very long discussion to go in-depth, but I will try to be as clear as possible without being too prolix.

Until no long ago it was a common thought that you only need 28 days to change a habit and to start getting new results. What I feel it's important to share with you it's that in my experience this is not entirely true, I found out that the time frame depends on too many factors to be generalized to any extent. I have seen people decide and change habits in a second and live the rest of their lives with those new habits. I have also seen people taking months to get to that same result.

For example, a person can be overweight for years without managing to change his food habits to lose weight. One day a health problem comes up and the doctor's diagnosis is either losing weight or putting life at risk. If the person in question prices life, he will change his food habits in no time according to the doctor's suggestions. The same example could fit for somebody that wants to quit smoking. So, urgency and reasons are definitely important in determining the time you need to get results.

Another very important element is how deeply is rooted the habit or the paradigm you need to override. You might have been exposed for years to false information, so may take 6 months or even a year to override these information with new ones that can give you new results.

So, if you know your goal and you know you want to reach it through visualization, start practicing and do it as often as you can. As for the question, "How long will it take", my answer is, "It depends". It takes the time that it takes. I know it may sound bad, but that's the truth and I want to be completely honest with you, I don't want to create false expectations.

That being said, in my experience people following this method start to see the first small changes in results within a month. The majority of people I have been working with start to see interesting results within 3 to 6 months of constantly applying this method. I also encountered a minority that took a year and over, but they got where they wanted to get.

Time flies anyway. One, two, or three years aren't such a long time, but they will pass anyway, so may just as well use them to build something important for your life.

Many people ask, "How long does it take?", but they never bother even starting, and I find this rather amusing. I can surely state that if you never start you will never get the chance to improve your life.

Remember, time flies anyway! I prefer using my time doing things that make my life better and better every day.

THE METHOD INTO PRACTICE

In this section, I would like to repeat how the visualization process works, so you can see very clearly in your mind how the changes take place thanks to this process.

We all have thoughts in our minds, all the time. Those thoughts keep running into our heads and the more we pay attention to them and we let them run free, the more powerful they get. Our thoughts get stronger and stronger, and when they connect with emotions their power increase, and their energy level becomes very high. When a thought is so full of energy and we keep feeding it, we express this thought into an action and actions give us results.

Unconsciously, this process takes place inside every one of us, all day, every day. It is through this process that we get our results in life.

When you apply visualization, you use this process to your advantage, to reach your goals and what you truly want in life.

So, the starting point is the answer to the question: "What goal do I want to reach?". The answer is the starting point of your visualization.

Now, find a peaceful place and relax. Take deep breaths, close your eyes and count from 10 to 0, allowing yourself to reach a relaxed and meditative state.

In this ideal state, start to build in your mind the image of your goal, see yourself as you already have achieved it. At this point, start to add as many details as possible. Add motions, smells, sounds, sensations, feelings, the right light. You are creating a mental film, the more detailed the movie will be, the more effective it will be. Try to imagine how you would feel about achieving your goal. Try to imagine the language and the words you would use to describe your amazing results and to compliment yourself. Keep adding all the details you feel like adding to make this movie perfect for you.

At this point, you should have a very clear picture of your goal on the screen of your mind. From that point of view try to look backward. What did you do to get there? What particular actions brought you exactly where you wanted to be? Think about it, with the help of your imagination. Then, see yourself doing those actions. See people complimenting you for your amazing success. See yourself in the environment you want to live in. Feel the great sensations of having achieved all that.

When you feel it's enough for that session, before opening your eyes, be grateful for all the good results you reached and for achieving your goal. Be grateful, now! Only then, you can open your eyes.

You can repeat this exercise as often as you want. If you understood the explanation I opened this section with, you also understood that this is a great way to keep your mind focused on good thoughts, to keep it focused on the things you want in your life so that soon they will express into new actions that will give new results. I can assure you that if just now you don't have the life you want it's because your mind is unconsciously focused on the things you don't want. Use visualization to consciously focus your mind on what you want as often as you can and enjoy the amazing results.

Let's Go A Little Deeper

I work with all sorts of people that want to achieve success in different areas of their life. When I first encounter them they wonder if this method can be applied in their area of interest.

In this section, I would like to give a quick look at the three major areas that people show the highest interest: business, fitness, and happiness. You can use visualization to improve any area of your life. I just want to go a little more in-depth in the ones, in my experience, the majority of people focus on.

Business

When business people first approach visualization, they usually come up with questions like, "How can visualization bring more customers into my business? I don't think that if I visualize more people they will just materialize into my store!"

I assume that if you have a business, you also have a product or a service that you want to sell to people. I also assume that you have a process in place to reach those people you want to sell your product to and a process to do the actual sale. The better this process is, the more people you will reach and the more sales you will do.

What do you need the visualization process for, then? You can start by visualizing your process to clarify your ideas, to get a better overview of the entire process, and to see how you could improve to get better results every day.

If you visualize your goal and you feel like you already achieved it, your head starts to unlock resources and you start to get new ideas to implement in your process. Visualization kick-starts your creative part so that you can start to see new solutions to improve your business.

Obviously, if a businessman thinks that he can sit on a sofa, do nothing but visualize money falling from the sky, and materialize that somehow, that's an absurd expectation.

What you can expect by practicing visualization for your business, it's to start seeing things from a different point of view. You will see what doesn't work, what needs improving and your daily actions to make things better will eventually give you amazing and successful results.

Sales

This subject is very close to the one we just discussed in the business section, but I want to analyze it in a separate section because I get a lot of salespeople that don't work for themselves and need to show results to keep their jobs and increase their wedges.

Salespeople usual question is, "How do I increase my sales with visualization? It's the other person that decides to buy or not!".

It's very true, it's the customer that decides if he wants to buy or not, but the customers chose depending on the sales presentation of the salesman. The salesman has the power to find interesting reasons for the customer to buy. He has the power to understand what influences the customer to buy or not. The salesman's attitude towards the customer is fundamental for his final choice.

As you can see, if you are a salesman there is a lot of stuff that you can visualize. You should start from your goal: close the sale. Then you should move backward. What kind of customer do you want to sell to? What questions should you ask them during your presentation? How should you answer their objections? How could you control the psychological and emotional aspects of the sale? How could you improve yourself as a salesman?

There are no sales for those that are not prepared to sell. It is the customer that decides to buy, but the salesman has to be prepared for this.

Basically, with visualization, you prepare yourself to sell because you keep rehearsing in your mind a lot of different and possible sales circumstances. Thanks to this rehearsal you will know what to do when a certain circumstance shows up. After all, you have already donut so many times (in your mind).

Use your visualization to see how prepared you are. Use it to rehearse your presentation and to try to understand what doesn't work and how to improve it. Use it to simulate eventual objections and how you would answer to those. Use it to understand how to control every situation, even when a difficult customer is making you feel uneasy. I recommend you to include in your visualizations a lot of happy customers signing your contracts, feel the feeling that you would feel in such a moment, see exactly what you did to get to that signature.

Remember that to sell you need a process. If you don't have one already you should build it even through visualization or use it to improve what you build. Just keep in mind that action is fundamental to materialize results.

Fitness

Those who want to get fitter, do better training sessions, or improve health usually express their doubt with sentences like, "I can't just sit down, visualize that I am slimmer, fitter, and healthier and I get all that like a miracle!"

Of course not, and we already discussed that in every circumstance. What can be amazingly beneficial to the results you wish to obtain it's to visualize yourself exactly as you want to be. See yourself as you had already achieved your goal and start to feel that way. Feel the satisfaction for achieving such an amazing result, or feel like you already won that competition you are training for if that's your goal. This way of visualizing will change your mental status and, consequently, your physical condition, in fact, we can accomplish something just if we can first see it in our mind.

If you don't see it in your mind, if you can't imagine it, you can't accomplish it. On the other hand, if you see yourself as an amazing athlete, you will face training and competitions like an amazing athlete.

Keep in mind to stay away from negative visualization. If you see yourself as fat and lazy, you won't even start any physical activity and you will spend your time eating junk food in front of your tv.

If you want to get healthier, win a competition, improve the way look, you might be working towards those goals with practical actions. Visualization will help improve the process you are following to get towards your goal because it improves your psychological aspect in the first place, and you should have understood by now how this is fundamental. It all starts in your mind.

For example, to improve your food regime you could visualize yourself eating healthy food, deeply enjoying it and feeling a lot better as a result. By practicing on those images and feelings you will condition your brain to think that you like salad more than you like a greasy cheeseburger and that will soon become your new habit to practice.

To get fitter or to prepare yourself for a competition, you could imagine yourself practicing your exercises in a better way than usual and with less effort. You should feel your muscles working as you were truly performing those exercises. You should see yourself winning the competition and how great you would feel in such a moment. You should see yourself looking at your image in the mirror with a toned and fit body and feel all the satisfaction and happiness for such a great result. Listen in your head to all the people cheering at your victory or complimenting you for your new amazing look.

Once again, stay on the couch won't get you any result, but by combining action and positive visualization you can achieve everything you want.

Happiness

Can I use visualization to reach happiness in life? Yes, yes, and yes!

To understand how to use visualization to achieve happiness, I need to make a preliminary remark. I hear all the time people saying, "I will be happy when that happens. I will be happy when I will get that thing. I can only be happy if...". Forget all the "Whens" and "Ifs", if you want to be happy, you have to be happy now. This is how happiness works.

You have to feel happy now, immediately, without anything happening. If you do, the world around you will totally change, because it will reflect your new attitude. Happiness is a state of mind, a mental attitude, that originates from your thoughts and expresses itself through your actions.

So, if you stick happy thoughts to your mind and block the negative junk, you will start expressing your positive feeling through your actions and your surrounding will change. It is truly like living in a different world you had never seen before.

Visualization's a great instrument to train your mind to feel happy before this or that. In a very calm and relaxed state, you should start to visualize yourself happy in that very moment, feel how amazing is to be in such a state. See yourself smiling, enjoying life, and as you do that and enjoy the sensation it brings to you, be thankful. The more you feel gratitude, the better you will feel and you will soon manifest all that good in your life.

Your thoughts and your actions determine your attitude. If you keep your mind busy with happy, healthy, and positive thoughts, you will be happy as a result. In that state, you will do good actions and that will make feel happiness and joy. This becomes a circle.

If you keep waiting on something outside you to happen to be happy, you will never be. I often hear people saying, "I will be happy as soon as I have enough money to buy that car, that bag, that pair of shoes,…". When they get, they feel just ok, because the best part was the trip to get there, the fact of being able to afford something so cool.

What do I mean by that? I mean that you create your happiness now, with what you think and with the images you hold into your mind. It has nothing to do with having this or that, or with certain things to happen.

Don't take me wrong, here! The achieve results it's beautiful and amazing. Everybody should have the ambition to reach higher results: a better car, better clothes, a bigger house, more money, an higher lifestyle, you name. It's an amazing sensation when you achieve those goals, but you can be happy now and all along your path. You don't need to wait to get there to be happy.

So, the way to use visualization to achieve happiness it's to open up your imagination and create beautiful images of yourself happy and joyful. During your day, even if you are not visualizing in that very moment, bring back to your mind these images and try to keep them in your mind as long as you can. Be happy now!

Being All That Said...

Even now that you know and understand the amazing power of visualization, you may have bad days. You may come to face difficult days, where you don't seem to see any result, or maybe you may just wake up in the morning with bad thoughts that you don't wish to have, but those negative thoughts keep following you all day long.

It could even be that that you are being badly influenced by your surroundings. Maybe you wish to live in a different place, in a different home, or find new friends to spend your time with, but you can't do any of those things yet and you get negative thoughts influenced by those circumstances.

When you get caught in any negative situation, all I can recommend is to practice visualization as often as you can, to keep switching your mind on positive and happy thoughts. See yourself already living the way you want to be and forget what surrounds you just now. See yourself as you already achieved the goals you want to achieve and forget the results you see just now around you. Make your mental pictures as vivid as possible. The more details you add to the scene, the more the visualization will change the way are feeling and the quality of your thoughts, so the outside negative world will fade away and you will soon materialize what you visualize.

If you wake up with negative thoughts, instead of spiraling down all day, just take 5 or 10 minutes for yourself and start visualizing your beautiful mental movie and that will immediately give your mind and your attitude a new orientation.

If you feel down because of the lack of good results, take an extra 5 or 10 minutes during your day to see on the screen of your mind the amazing results you want as if you already have achieved them. If the results that you wish to materialize in your life come from your business or your job, see yourself while you are working on your projects happily and full of energy. Visualize your results. If it's money you wish to get from your job so you can improve your lifestyle, see yourself doing stuff at work that will bring that money to you. See that money as already in your pockets. These beautiful pictures will help you find motivation and good ideas while you are working and those things will soon materialize what you want into your life.

So, when you have feelings and sensations that you don't like, you should use visualization to get out of that spiral of negativity. Use the positive images you created to keep you motivated and to lead you to the life you really want.

Hold those images on the screen of your mind every time you can, impress them, keep bringing them up and keep playing your movie on the screen of your mind. You may feel like a daydreamer and that's good. You have to persevere in visualizing what you want until it starts materializing into your psychical world. Keep practicing actions in your mind, they will find expression through your body, and then you will achieve your goal.

Let's See A Few Examples

I will never stop repeating how important it is to act on what you visualize, in fact too many people misunderstand this fundamental part. Start acting now, get moving! Start putting into practice what you visualize.

Now, many people forgot how to use imagination so, here are a few examples that you could use as suggestions to awake your imagination. You should see those examples as starting points to help you begin somewhere. I choose three examples from questions I often receive from my usual clients.

GOAL: EMPLOY A NEW EFFICIENT MEMBER OF STAFF

A suggestion of visualization: You should start picturing this person on the screen of your mind with full details. What kind of characteristics should this person have? Should he (she) be reliable? Precise? Creative? A long-hours worker? What is it that you require? You could even add physical details. Should he have a nice and tidy look? Do you need a good-looking receptionist? Do you want a nerd that stays all day attached to his computer? Build the clearest picture possible. Once you have your ideal employee ready, start imagining how you found him. Did you advertise the job posting online or in the local newspaper? Did you ask at the jobcentre? Visualize exactly how you found your ideal employee and visualize the exact interview. What did you ask? What replies did you wish to get and why? Then, picture in your mind the training phase. For example, see your new employee as he patiently listens to what he gets taught, see him listening very attentively, see him eager to learn. Imagine him doing the correct way the job you hired him for, picture how much he likes it, and how happy he is in working for you. You should be very present in your visualization. See yourself very happy to have found such a good worker, exactly the kind of person you wanted. Keep adding details and practice this visualization as often as you can, while you start posting the job just as you visualized it and you start the job interviews.

GOAL: SELL A CERTAIN PRODUCT OR SERVICE

A suggestion of visualization: Let's imagine that you want to sell a psychical product in a psychical store. I would suggest you start picturing yourself in your store and a lot of customers coming in. Start to see yourself talking to them. What questions could you ask to better understand how to present to them the product you wish to sell? Then you could picture them asking questions to you about that product, how would you answer those questions? Start creating your movie and rehearse a situation that you very likely will come to face. Remember to involve feelings and sensations. For example, imagine how well you feel when you realize how much you impressed them with your answers, what good impression you are making, and how happy they are to interact with you. Feel the trust in yourself growing according to this positive outcome. Imagine yourself doing your sale presentation and your customers' reaction to it, they understand the product, how useful is for them and immediate trust starts building up between you and each one of your customers. Keep adding as many details as possible. Visualize a few more final questions, see your customers happy to buy your product, and feel your joy for how well you conducted each transaction.

Rehearse this visualization as often as you can and see how helpful it will be when facing your customers every day at work.

GOAL: IMPROVE YOUR PHYSICAL SHAPE

A suggestion of visualization: Start building in your mind the exact image of the body you would like to achieve. For example, imagine your body toned and fit, healthy and full of energy, slim, and with a few muscles well on view. Remember the importance of details, so create a very precise picture. Then see yourself looking around for information on how you could achieve such results and applying them. Visualize yourself practicing all the new habits to achieve such results. Imagine yourself waking up earlier in the morning to do some exercises before going to work. See yourself eating in a better way, healthier food, and decent quantities. Imagine yourself conscious of the fact that you like healthy food a lot more than you like junk food. See yourself taking care of the quality and quantity of your sleep. Along with the details add as many feelings and sensations as possible. Imagine how you feel with that exact body you always dreamed of, and that now you achieved. Imagine your joy in a clothes shop buying everything a couple of sizes less than you always had before. Start hearing all the compliments from your friends and family and feel proud of what you achieved. Keep adding details.

Rehearse this visualization as often as you can and try to use it during your day when you decide what time to set your alarm clock or when you decide what time you go to sleep, or every time you sit in front of something to eat.

Chapter 9:

How To Use Affirmations To Improve Your Visualization

Now that I explained in full detail the process, I would like to give a few tips and some tools that can help you improve the work you are starting to do on yourself.

During my studies and my various attempts to improve the method, the practice that helped me the most to keep my mind focused and to bring back the images of my visualization during my day, has been to repeat affirmations.

When you do an affirmation you are declaring a certain idea or position that creates an image on the screen of your mind. You unconsciously do that pretty often. Every time you say, "I am not feeling well today", for example, you are affirming that to yourself and you are creating an image of your poor state. The more you repeat that sentence, the more you will see the associated picture to the screen of your mind and the more your body will adapt to correspond to that image. The result is that you keep feeling worst and worst.

If you say just once that you don't feel well, it may not be such big damage, you turn your mind in another direction and no harm is done, but continuous repletion can be a great danger. The danger could be even worst if you attach any emotion to that image of discomfort.

I didn't use the "I am not feeling well" example just out of chance, but because I am often surrounded by people that, instead of using the power of positive affirmation, waste their time picturing and repeating how badly they feel, how bad things are going. The only result that I see them getting is that they look worst every time I meet them.

If a person doesn't feel well, this person should immediately seek help and see a doctor. When I mention this I often get answered that they have to think about it, but they keep complaining about this and that.

I can assure you that out there it's full of people of this kind, and if you are not one of them you can easily be a victim of one of those people. So, if you just realized that you are a complainer, stop right away. On the other hand, if you realized you are surrounded by complainers, keep away from them.

You most probably are in one of these two situations, if you haven't yet reached your goal. I would like you to focus your attention on the fact that this same thing that can be an obstacle, used properly can be your greatest help.

Think about all those people that are always smiling, cheery, happy to be alive. They always look beautiful and bright like a burst of sunshine. You can bet that those people keep doing the right positive affirmation to themselves, and they surely keep well away from grumpy complainers.

They always smile, no matter what, but I am pretty sure that they have bad days too, and problems now and then. It's life! We all have happy moments and sad ones, problems and solutions, the difference is made by the power we give to the negative events.

This is why you have to create positive sentences, positive affirmations that will always keep you focused on the positive side, on the beautiful things, and on the goal you want to achieve. Once you have created them and each sentence has its image, keep repeating them to yourself, both in your mind and out loud.

I can share a few examples, just in case you are still working on your imagination.

"I like myself so much!"

"I am so happy and I feel so good!"

"I am so grateful to have such a healthy body and I keep it in good shape exercising daily!"

"I make more and more money every day!"

"I always feel happy and full of joy!"

I know all this may sound a bit weird but, after reading all the previous chapters, you should have understood how easy it is to influence our mind. Repetition is the element that does the majority of the job. What we keep hearing, what we continuously see, the images that run frequently on the screen of our minds, our internal dialogue, and the affirmations and the statements we keep repeating to ourselves, all these elements influence our minds and our lives.

If you don't do this process voluntarily, you will be a victim of somebody else's process and you won't definitely like such a circumstance. You might be surrounded by negative people repeating their bad statements because they don't have the habit to treat well themselves. For example, you could have a colleague moaning all day about the job he hates. Then you might go home to find a partner complaining about sadness and poor health. When you go out with friends the main topic of discussion is the lack of something and not having enough money to do all they want. If you don't protect yourself you become a victim of all those bad and negative affirmations, that don't belong to you because they have nothing to do with your goal.

You can protect yourself with your own positive affirmations. Run them through your mind or even out loud, as longs you don't leave any space for somebody else's negative statements.

These positive affirmations will make your visualizations a lot stronger and more powerful. While you are visualizing a certain part of your goal, a section very rich in details that you can see, hear, feel, smell, and touch, link this image to a positive statement. Every time you will repeat that affirmation during your day, the related image will appear on the screen of your mind. The more the images you visualize stay on the screen of your mind, the sooner your body will find a way to express them.

For example, if you want a new job, create the image in full detail and see yourself in the image saying, "I am so happy to have this new marvelous job!". Repeat it during your day and the image you created of your new job will appear on the screen of your mind.

As I said you can repeat your affirmations either in your mind or out loud. I know you might feel strange about saying them aloud, but it's a very powerful exercise. I repeat them aloud at least 20 or 30 times in the morning and again before going to bed, you could do it under the shower if you don't want to be heard. You should also repeat them during your day. You need to develop the habit to repeat your affirmations and writing them down could be a useful method. Handwrite your statement a few times and keep that sheet of paper on your working surface. Every time you will catch it with your eyes, your mind will remember to repeat your affirmation. I repeat my affirmations every time I can because I know very well the enormous power they hold.

I must underline that I find very useful the repetition method through handwriting. I practice written repetition of my affirmations on a daily basis. I have a notebook dedicated to that and I make sure to have a dedicated space of time for this exercise.

I use this same writing method to repeat my visualizations, too. I write down a precise description of my visualization in full detail, just so I do an extra daily repetition of the visualization of my goal.

I even have a trick you might find very useful, especially at the beginning. Use the voice recorder app on your mobile phone and record a few minutes of yourself saying out loud your positive affirmations, then listen to them (headphones on if you feel more comfortable) in loop mode as often as you can.

All these exercises are meant to make you stay with your goal as often as possible and to keep your mind away from what you don't want. This is how you reach a goal.

Chapter 10:

What To Do Now

Well, congratulations! You made it to the end.

Your first step now is to try to apply and put into practice what you read in the previous chapters.

Find a quiet spot, sit or lie down and relax. Breath slowly and start exercising to create images in your mind of things that you want and that make you feel good. See the images of the goal you want to achieve or how you want to improve a certain situation, so you can start to influence your subconscious mind.

Another step you should take it's to read this book again, more than once. It's not very long, but I can assure you that I wrote very important concepts and ideas that can truly change your entire life. By now you should also have understood the importance of repetition.

I read each book at least three times because repetition is important, but this is not the only reason. See, what happens is that when I read something, a word or a concept makes me think and I drift away from what I am reading without even noticing. Because of this "distraction", I end up losing very important parts of what I am reading.

When I read each book three times, every time I notice a sentence, a concept, or an idea that I didn't see the previous time. It's almost like reading a new book and I get new knowledge and new ideas.

You might have experienced something similar when watching a movie more than once and discovered scenes that you had never seen before. Reading a book more than once it's a very similar experience.

I know it could seem a strange recommendation to read the same book so many times, but that feeling of strangeness comes from the fact that we have never been taught to do so, we never developed that habit. At least, this was true for me. Nobody ever thought me to read a book more than once. I discovered this habit by reading books of smart people that recommended doing so. I tried it and now I know the huge impact this habit can have I couldn't do without. This is why I am passing the advice to you.

As a further step, I would suggest you an amusing exercise that will help you develop your imagination and also to keep your goal in front of your eyes. I call this exercise *"Visualization Wall"*.

Get a fair amount of magazines and start scouting for images that are connected with your goal. Cut those images, glue them to a board, and place that board in good sight in a place where you spend a lot of time.

Cut the picture of the house you would like to live in and a photo of you standing in the same context. Cut the image of the car you want to drive and place your face as the driver's face. Do the same for as many aspects as you can. Chose the clothes you want to wear, the jewels you want, the bags or the tech gadgets. Cut the perfect holiday location and the place where you would like to work. Remember to add a photo of yourself in each situation. If your goal is to lose weight and have a fit body, look for pictures of models with a shape similar to the one you want to achieve, cut those photos and substitute your face with the one of the models. Place the board with your dream life or goal on the fridge door, on your closet, anywhere you get to see it all the time. You could even do more than one board and place them around your house in place of your usual paintings. The more you will be surrounded by those images the more you will stay focused on your goal and on the thing you want.

Last but not least, you should consider this book just a starting point. Start to explore the ideas that aroused your interests the most. Look for books on those subjects, articles, or videos. Find related subjects to go even deeper, as to build a useful cultural and intellectual baggage.

This is what I usually do myself. When I meet an interesting idea, I start to go deeper to understand better what I read. This research makes you a richer person, you are your best investment. Sometimes I go back on time with books from 1800 or the starting of 1900. I like to find original editions and it's very interesting to read them, even if sometimes a little hard to understand. I find it interesting to discover how people thought about a certain thing so many years ago versus how we see it now. I must also admit that many things are very actual even after such a long time, so go in-depth and sometimes back to the origins of some ideas.

I hope you find all this as inspiring as it is for me. If you found useful what you read in these pages, if you enjoyed taking this journey together, if you already started to apply what you read and you got your first results, I recommend you to share all those information with the people you recon could benefit and enjoy this practice. Share it with anybody that can take advantage of those information.

Thank you for staying with me to the end of this book, now's time to act!

I wish you a happy and healthy life!

Made in United States
Troutdale, OR
04/02/2024

18878191R00072